Red-Eyed Tree Frogs

written and photographed
by John Netherton

Lerner Publications Company • Minneapolis, Minnesota

For my son Jason ("Frog") Netherton and his wife, Joy

Thanks to our series consultant, Sharyn Fenwick, elementary science/math specialist. Mrs. Fenwick was the winner of the National Science Teachers Association 1991 Distinguished Teaching Award. She also was the recipient of the Presidential Award for Excellence in Math and Science Teaching, representing the state of Minnesota at the elementary level in 1992.

Additional photographs are reproduced through the courtesy of: © Leroy Simon/Visuals Unlimited, p. 9; © S. R. Maglione/The National Audubon Society/Photo Researchers, Inc., p. 10; © Michael and Patricia Fogden, pp. 11, 35, 42; © Alan D. Carey/The National Audubon Society/Photo Researchers, Inc., pp. 13, 40; © Michael P. Turco, p. 16; © Carrol Henderson, p. 18; © Renee Lynn/The National Audubon Society/Photo Researchers, Inc., p. 21; © Kevin Schafer, p. 41.

This series was conceived by Ruth Berman and designed by Steve Foley. Series editor is Joelle Riley.

Lerner Publications Company
A division of Lerner Publishing Group
241 First Avenue North
Minneapolis, MN 55401 U.S.A.

Website address: www.lernerbooks.com

Library of Congress Cataloging-in-Publication Data

Netherton, John.
    Red-eyed tree frogs / written and photographed by John
  Netherton.
      p.   cm. — (Early bird nature books)
    Summary: Presents information about the physical
  description, habitat, and life cycle of this colorful species of
  tree frog that is native to the Central American rain forest.
    ISBN 0-8225-3037-6 (alk. paper)
    1. Red-eyed tree frog—Juvenile literature. [1. Tree frogs.
  2. Frogs.] I. Title. II. Series.
  QL668.E24N48 2001
  597.8'7—dc21   99-38915

Manufactured in the United States of America
1 2 3 4 5 6 - JR - 06 05 04 03 02 01

Contents

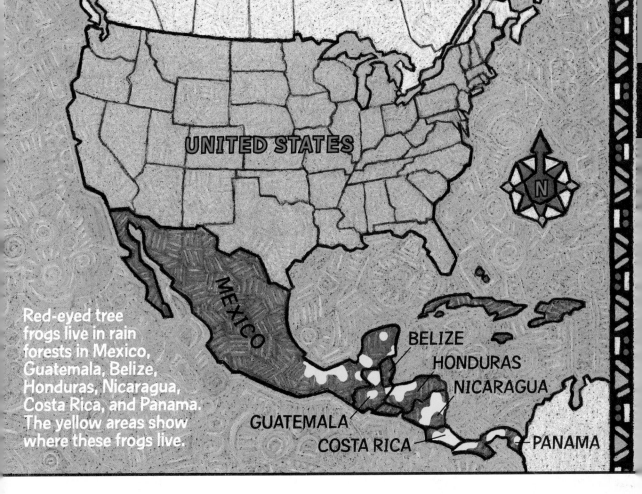

Red-eyed tree frogs live in rain forests in Mexico, Guatemala, Belize, Honduras, Nicaragua, Costa Rica, and Panama. The yellow areas show where these frogs live.

UNITED STATES

MEXICO

BELIZE
HONDURAS
NICARAGUA
GUATEMALA
COSTA RICA
PANAMA

Be a Word Detective

Can you find these words as you read about the life of the red-eyed tree frog? Be a detective and try to figure out what they mean. You can turn to the glossary on page 46 for help.

amphibians	endangered	predators
canopy	extinct	rain forests
cluster	metamorphosis	tadpole
cold-blooded	nocturnal	vocal sac

5

Chapter 1

Red-eyed tree frogs are very colorful. Where do most tree frogs live?

A Beautiful Frog

This frog is amazing. It is lime green. It has blue stripes, orange feet, and big red eyes. It is a red-eyed tree frog.

The world has more than 600 species, or kinds, of tree frogs. Most species of tree frogs live in trees. But some species live on the ground. They live on plants or under logs. Red-eyed tree frogs live in trees.

There are almost 4,000 species of frogs in the world. About 600 species are tree frogs.

Tree frogs are amphibians (am-FIH-bee-uhnz). Frogs, toads, and salamanders are all amphibians. Amphibians are animals who have moist skin. Amphibian babies live in water. They breathe underwater, like fish. When they grow up, they live on land. Then they breathe air.

Red-eyed tree frogs start life in water on the ground. When they grow up, they live in trees.

This is a rain forest. Central America has many rain forests like this one.

Red-eyed tree frogs live in rain forests. A rain forest is a thick, wet forest. Rain forests get more than 100 inches of rain a year. The deep end of a swimming pool is about 100 inches deep. The rain forests where red-eyed tree frogs live are in Central America. These rain forests are warm all year long.

To cool off, a red-eyed tree frog hops into the shade.

Like all amphibians, red-eyed tree frogs are cold-blooded. This means the temperature inside their bodies matches the temperature around them. Since the temperature is always warm where red-eyed tree frogs live, the frogs stay warm. If a red-eyed tree frog gets too warm, it cools off in the shade.

People are warm-blooded animals. The temperature inside our bodies does not match the temperature around us. It stays the same no matter where we are.

The rain forests of Central America are always warm.

Chapter 2

A red-eyed tree frog could sit in your hand. Can a small red-eyed tree frog jump from one big tree to the next?

Life in the Rain Forest

Red-eyed tree frogs are small. They are just 3 to 5 inches long when they are adults. The rain forests of Central America where they live are huge. But those huge forests are the perfect home for them.

A red-eyed tree frog spends most of its life in the rain forest canopy (KAN-uh-pee). The canopy is the highest branches of the trees. The branches spread out and touch each other. Red-eyed tree frogs can jump easily from tree to tree.

This is a rain forest canopy. The treetops are like a roof over the forest.

Red-eyed tree frogs can climb easily, too. That is because they have suction cups on their toes. The suction cups grip tightly. They help a frog hold onto tree bark, branches, and leaves.

The rain forests of Central America do not have a cold winter and a hot summer. But they do have a wet season and a dry season.

The suction cups on a tree frog's toes are sticky. They help the frog stick to slippery sticks and leaves.

The wet season begins in May. Rain falls almost every day. Rain drips down tree trunks. It runs onto branches and leaves. It collects in pools on the ground.

Most frogs need to stay moist. They need to soak up water. They soak up water through their skin. A red-eyed tree frog can easily find the water it needs during the wet season.

This tree stump has rainwater in it.

This frog is sitting on a rain forest plant.

The dry season begins in December. Only a little rain falls. The pools of water on the ground dry up. The water on branches and leaves dries. When this happens, a red-eyed tree frog's skin becomes waxy. The waxy skin helps the frog stay moist.

Chapter 3

Red-eyed tree frogs are awake at night. What do we call animals who are active at night?

Night and Day

Red-eyed tree frogs are nocturnal (nok-TUR-nuhl). Nocturnal animals are active at night.

At night, red-eyed tree frogs look for food. They are predators (PREH-duh-turz). Predators are animals who hunt and eat other animals.

Red-eyed tree frogs see things that are far away better than they see things that are near. This frog may be looking for insects to eat.

Red-eyed tree frogs hunt and eat insects. The frogs can easily hunt at night. They see well in the dark. They can see tiny insects quickly flying by.

To hunt, a red-eyed tree frog walks around slowly. It looks for insects. When the frog sees an insect, it jumps toward the insect. The frog quickly sticks out its tongue. The insect gets stuck on the tongue. Then the frog eats the insect.

Red-eyed tree frogs sometimes eat butterflies like this one. A rain forest has lots of insects.

A red-eyed tree frog climbs to a high place to sleep.

When day comes, a red-eyed tree frog climbs to a high branch. It sleeps on the branch or under a leaf. It sleeps in a different place each night.

This red-eyed tree frog is sleeping.

Birds, lizards, and snakes all hunt and eat red-eyed tree frogs. So when a red-eyed tree frog sleeps, it hides. The frog pulls its legs close to its body. It tucks in its toes. It closes its red eyes. Only the frog's green skin shows. That way, predators cannot easily see it.

A red-eyed tree frog sleeps alone all day.
When night comes, it wakes and hunts again.

This snake could eat a red-eyed tree frog. But the frogs are hard to see when they are sleeping.

Chapter 4

This is a male red-eyed tree frog. He is calling. When a male calls, he looks like he has a balloon in his throat. Why do male red-eyed tree frogs call?

Starting a Family

When the wet season begins, a male red-eyed tree frog finds a female. Then the male and the female start a family.

To find a female, a male calls. The call sounds like "chock." Many males call at the same time. The rain forest gets very noisy!

Only male red-eyed tree frogs can call. Only males have a vocal sac (VOH-kuhl sak). A vocal sac is a small bag inside a male frog's throat. The male uses his vocal sac to make sound.

Female red-eyed tree frogs do not call. They listen.

A male red-eyed tree frog starts to call as night begins. He climbs downward as he calls. Sometimes he finds a female. Sometimes a female hears him and comes to him. The female is bigger than the male.

Like all male tree frogs, this one has a vocal sac in his throat. This frog is not calling, so the vocal sac is flat.

This female red-eyed tree frog is carrying a male on her back.

The male climbs onto the female's back.
The female carries the male downward. She
climbs down to a low branch.

This female red-eyed tree frog is laying eggs.

Then the female lays eggs. She lays many eggs in a group called a cluster. She lays the cluster on the underside of a leaf. The eggs in the cluster are covered with goop. The goop helps the cluster stick to the leaf.

Then the female carries the male all the way down to the ground. They jump into a pool of water. They soak up some of the water.

These frogs are soaking up water. The female needs lots of water to make goop for her eggs.

The goop that covers a cluster helps the cluster stick to a leaf.

Then they climb back to the cluster of eggs on the branch. The female lays another cluster. The frogs repeat this many times.

When all the female's eggs are laid, the male and female frogs leave. Red-eyed tree frogs do not stay near their eggs. They do not take care of their young.

Chapter 5

These eggs are changing. What is growing inside them?

Life as a Tadpole

Inside each egg is a tiny tadpole. A tadpole is a baby frog. As a tadpole grows, it starts to spin and swim inside the egg.

In about one week, the egg bursts open. The tadpole pours out. It falls into the pool under its leaf.

These tadpoles are hatching. The tadpoles in a cluster often hatch at the same time.

Tadpoles wiggle and flip around until they fall off the leaf.

Sometimes a tadpole gets stuck. It wiggles and twists until it slides off, into the pool. Sometimes a tadpole lands on dry ground. Then it flips around until it lands in the pool. Tadpoles cannot live outside water.

Tadpoles are made for life in the water. They are shaped like fish. They swim like fish, too. They can breathe underwater, like fish.

A tadpole's tail is always moving.

Tadpoles live in water on the rain forest floor.

A tadpole eats algae (AL-jee). Algae are tiny plants that grow in water. A tadpole also eats leaves and plants that fall into its pool.

A tadpole swims in its pool for several weeks. Slowly, the tadpole changes. This change is called a metamorphosis (met-uh-MOR-fuh-sis).

You can see tiny back legs growing on this tadpole.

During metamorphosis, the tadpole grows legs. First it grows two back legs. Next it grows two front legs. The tadpole also grows lungs for breathing air.

The tadpole still has a tail. Its eyes are gold or brown, not red. But mostly, it looks like a red-eyed tree frog.

A red-eyed tree frog's eyes turn red soon after it leaves the water.

This young frog's tail will shrink. The tail will be gone in a few days.

Finally the tadpole is ready to leave the water. It climbs out of its pool and hops to a tree. It climbs up the tree to the rain forest canopy.

Chapter 6

This bulldozer is clearing land in a rain forest. Why do people cut down rain forest trees?

Frogs and People

Central America has huge rain forests. But many trees are cut down every day. People cut down the trees to make room for farms.

When this happens, many animals lose their homes. Red-eyed tree frogs have to live in rain forests. When an animal does not have a home, it dies.

Some species of frogs are extinct. This means all of the frogs of one species are dead. Some species are endangered. They are in danger of becoming extinct.

When trees are cut down, many animals lose their homes.

These children are visiting a rain forest in Costa Rica.

Red-eyed tree frogs are not extinct. They are not endangered. They still have places to live. People are helping to save places for red-eyed tree frogs to live. In some schools, children raise money to buy rain forest land. No one can cut down trees on that land.

We can all help to save the world's beautiful rain forests. That way, a beautiful, red-eyed frog will always have a place to jump and climb and call.

We can all help to save places for this beautiful frog to live.

On Sharing a Book

As you know, adults greatly influence a child's attitude toward reading. When a child sees you read, or when you share a book with a child, you're sending a message that reading is important. Show the child that reading a book together is important to you. Find a comfortable, quiet place. Turn off the television and limit other distractions like telephone calls.

Be prepared to start slowly. Take turns reading parts of this book. Stop and talk about what you're reading. Talk about the photographs. You may find that much of the shared time is spent discussing just a few pages. This discussion time is valuable for both of you, so don't move through the book too quickly. If the child begins to lose interest, stop reading. Continue sharing the book at another time. When you do pick up the book again, be sure to revisit the parts you have already read. Most importantly, enjoy the book!

Be a Vocabulary Detective

You will find a word list on page 5. Words selected for this list are important to the understanding of the topic of this book. Encourage the child to be a word detective and search for the words as you read the book together. Talk about what the words mean and how they are used in the sentence. Do any of these words have more than one meaning? You will find these words defined in a glossary on page 46.

What about Questions?

Use questions to make sure the child understands the information in this book. Here are some suggestions:

What did this paragraph tell us? What does this picture show? What do you think we'll learn about next? How many kinds of tree frogs are there? Where do red-eyed tree frogs live? Could a red-eyed tree frog live in your backyard? Why/Why not? How are red-eyed tree frogs like people? How are they different? What do red-eyed tree frogs eat? How do red-eyed tree frogs find their food? How does a red-eyed tree frog sleep? How is a tadpole different from an adult red-eyed tree frog? What do you think it's like being a red-eyed tree frog? What is your favorite part of the book? Why?

If the child has questions, don't hesitate to respond with questions of your own like: What do *you* think? Why? What is it that you don't know? If the child can't remember certain facts, turn to the index.

Introducing the Index

The index is an important learning tool. It helps readers get information quickly without searching throughout the whole book. Turn to the index on page 47. Choose an entry such as *eggs* and ask the child to use the index to find out where a red-eyed tree frog lays its eggs. Repeat this exercise with as many entries as you like. Ask the child to point out the differences between an index and a glossary. (The index helps readers find information quickly, while the glossary tells readers what words mean.)

Where in the World?

Many plants and animals found in the Early Bird Nature Books series live in parts of the world other than the United States. Encourage the child to find the places mentioned in this book on a world map or globe. Take time to talk about climate, terrain, and how you might live in such places.

All the World in Metric!

Although our monetary system is in metric units (based on multiples of 10), the United States is one of the few countries in the world that does not use the metric system of measurement. Here are some conversion activities you and the child can do using a calculator:

WHEN YOU KNOW:	MULTIPLY BY:	TO FIND:
feet	0.3048	meters
inches	2.54	centimeters
gallons	3.787	liters
pounds	0.454	kilograms

Activities

Make up a story about red-eyed tree frogs. Be sure to include information from this book. Draw or paint pictures to illustrate your story.

Pretend you're a red-eyed tree frog. Go to a playground. Climb to the top of a slide or to the top of a jungle gym. What is it like to be up high? Would you like to spend most of your life in such a high place? What do you think it is like to be a red-eyed tree frog and live in the tops of trees?

Go to a zoo, nature center, or neighborhood pond to see frogs, toads, salamanders, and other amphibians. How are red-eyed tree frogs similar to these animals? How are they different?

Glossary

amphibians (am-FIH-bee-uhnz)—cold-blooded animals with backbones who spend part of their lives in water and the rest of their lives on land

canopy (KAN-uh-pee)—the top part of a forest

cluster—a group of eggs

cold-blooded—having a body temperature that matches the outside temperature

endangered—having only a few of a kind of animal still living

extinct—having no members of a kind of animal still living

metamorphosis (met-uh-MOR-fuh-sis)—the change from egg to tadpole to adult frog

nocturnal (nok-TUR-nuhl)—awake and active at night

predators (PREH-duh-turz)—animals who hunt and eat other animals

rain forests—very thick forests where a lot of rain falls

tadpole—a young frog

vocal sac (VOH-kuhl sak)—the part of a male frog's body that he uses to make sound

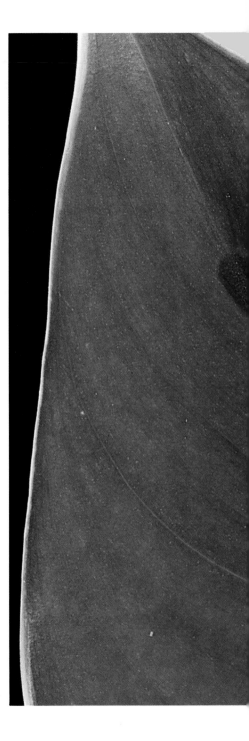

Index

Pages listed in **bold** type refer to photographs.

The Early Bird Nature Books Series